THE LITTLE BLIND SHEPHERD

A CHRISTMAS MIRACLE

To Joseph,

Kay Hall
Christmas 2014

Kay Hall

Houston Hall
PUBLISHING, LLC.

"For unto you is born this day in the city of David a Saviour, which is Christ the Lord. And this shall be a sign unto you; Ye shall find the babe wrapped in swaddling clothes, lying in a manger. And suddenly there was with the angel a multitude of the heavenly host praising God, and saying, Glory to God in the highest, and on earth peace, good will toward men."

– Luke 2:11-14

Houston Hall

PUBLISHING, LLC.
Marietta, Georgia

Copyright © 2014 by Houston Hall Publishing, LLC

Printed in the United States of America

10 9 8 7 6 5 4 3 2   0 9 2 5 1 4

ISBN: 978-0-9908153-0-3

Library of Congress Control Number: 2014951284

♾ This paper meets the requirements of ANSI/NISO Z39.48-1992 (Permanence of Paper)

In Loving Dedication to
Jimel "Jinks" Corley Olson
and
Vicki Olson Harshbarger

This book belongs to:

A little lad of Bethlehem is
coming down the street;
The sun shines warmly on his
smiling face, so young and sweet.

"A worthy lad," the folk of
Bethlehem are heard to say.
He brightens every heart that sees
him skipping home each day.

For though his path upon the
cobbled stones is sure and straight,
And though he knows each voice that
calls from shop or garden gate,

And though his laughter fills the air
proclaiming peace of mind,
The brave and joyful little lad
of Bethlehem is blind.

With here a step and there a turn,
his journey soon is past.
Someone listens for his voice...
ah, here he is at last!

"Mother, dear, I'm home," he calls
while bursting through the door.
Mira's arms are open wide;
her son is home once more.

Though she is mother of three
older sons, all tall and strong,
Little Josh, her special one,
can fill her heart with song.

"Are my brothers coming?
Has the sun begun to fade?
You do remember, Mother,
the promise that you made:

That I could go with them
tonight and help to tend the sheep?
It surely is a lovely night;
I know I couldn't sleep!

I want to be a shepherd, too.
Please, Mother, let me go!
Reuben, Malachi, and John
will keep me safe, I know."

"Hush, now, Josh, so many questions!
You will drive me wild."
But Mira's heart was stirred by
the excitement of the child.

Should she let him go
unto the hillside with the sheep?
Many dangers lurk within
the darkness, still and deep.

But darkness is no stranger
to the son she holds so dear;
For him it is a constant friend
and holds no special fear.

Heavy steps are heard outside;
familiar voices ring.
Mira hears the laughter and
the happy song they sing.

Reuben, Malachi, and John
are home for supper, too.
Little Josh jumps up and down;
his joy is born anew.

The happy boy cannot contain
himself; he runs to greet
The stalwart brothers who
are heroes in his
heart so sweet.

The oldest of the handsome
brothers tousles Josh's hair.
He picks him up with joy
and throws him high into
the air.

"Oh, Malachi," the mother
cries, "you'll surely hurt the
child." But he ignores
her pleading, for he
knows her heart
has smiled.

Now Josh is safely down and
hopping gaily on the floor.
He asks the questions of his
brothers he had asked before:

"Reuben, can I go with you
to tend the sheep tonight?
Malachi, you said the moon
would soon be full and bright.

John, I want so much to go,
I'm not afraid at all!"
The brothers' hearts were
tender toward the boy,
both blind and small.

John said, "Yes, come with us,
for we promised that you could."
"Oh, my sons," spoke Mira,
"do you really think he should?"

       "Now, Mother, we will keep
him safe," said brother Malachi.
Mira then gave up her fight and
breathed a gentle sigh.

       Reuben said, "Before we start
to make the journey there,
Could we have our latkes?
I'm as hungry as a bear!"

The little lad was even more
excited when, at last,
The family had eaten, and
the evening meal was past.

       "Hurry, hurry, can't we go?
I'm ready if you are.
I'm going to be a shepherd!
Is the journey very far?"

The cheerful band of brothers
bade their mother fond farewell.
She smiled bravely, but from her
eye a single teardrop fell.

Oh, how she loved the little boy
without the gift of sight.
She would surely pray for him
throughout the lonely night.

The troupe of young men started
out; the night was cool and clear.
Josh's lilting laughter
was a true delight to hear.

He held the hand of Malachi,
and Reuben walked beside.
John was close behind the three
and keeping gentle stride.

"Hurry, John, don't lag behind,"
the boy was heard to say.
"I'm so anxious to be there!
We must be on our way."

The older brothers' hearts were
happy just to hear the voice
Of little Josh; his happiness
made each of them rejoice.

"Patience, patience, little man.
It isn't very far."
Then Reuben suddenly exclaimed,
"Just look at that new star!

I've never seen one quite so big
or one that shines so bright."
Malachi said, "Reuben,
I believe for once you're right."

John stopped in his tracks
to gaze into the twilight sky.
No doubt, it was a truly brilliant
star that shone on high.

It seemed to set the sky
ablaze with effervescent fire.
It held the viewers captive
as its majesty rose higher.

Little Josh was listening to
the chatter of the three,
But as he could not share the
scene, he called impatiently,

"Brothers, we will never,
ever reach the meadow far,
If you stop along the way
to count each distant star!"

The brothers laughed,
returning their
attention to the one
They loved so much;
they did not mean to
spoil his night of fun.

"Don't worry, little
lad," said John, "for we
will soon be there.
The sheep are waiting
just for you to give
them special care.

Come climb upon my
shoulders, and we will be on
our way."
The little boy was lifted
up as he sang out, "Hurray!"

The band of brothers traveled
on beneath the star so bright.
Soon, their journey ended,
and the meadow was in sight.

Josh could hear the gentle sounds
of flocks upon the hill.
"Quiet now," said Malachi,
"don't frighten them; be still."

Little Josh stood silent, but
his heart beat loud with joy.
Tonight, at last, he had his
wish, to be a shepherd boy.

He took the hand of John
and walked toward the gentle sound
Of bleating lambs, and soon a
soft and furry head was found.

Josh reached out and touched
the softness of the woolly sheep.
"Come," said John, "we will rest
a while; the creatures need to sleep."

The brothers and the little lad sat
down upon the ground.
The gentle crying of the sheep
was now the only sound.

The little shepherd hoped to
stay awake throughout the night,
But soon his eyes grew heavy,
sleepy eyes which had no sight.

He had been so brave and
fearless coming to the wild!
The brothers looked with tender
love upon the sleeping child.

The brilliant star rose higher,
and the midnight hour came.
Malachi and John kept watch,
and Reuben did the same.

The night was hushed and clear
and still, and earth her rest did take,
When suddenly his brother's
shout brought little Josh awake.

The sky was bright as
noonday and was filled
with blinding light.
The band of hearty
shepherds cowered
now in dreadful fright!

"What is it?" cried the
shepherd boy who could
not see the sky.
He was clinging fearfully
to John and Malachi.

His brothers could not say a
word; he heard another voice.
It was an angel sent from God
to make the earth rejoice.

The angel said, "Fear not,
I bring you joyful news
this morn. For unto you in
Bethlehem, a Savior now is
born.

He is Christ the Lord, the
Son of God who reigns above.
Go unto the manger there
to find God's gift of love."

As the shepherds listened,
many angels' voices sang
In praise to God; it seemed to
Josh that all the
heavens rang.

Then the angels went away and
once again the night
Was hushed and calm and beautiful,
and still the star shone bright.

It seemed to beckon unto
them, but it was Josh who said,
"Let us go, my brothers,
we must find the manger bed!"

The brothers laughed in sweet
relief, agreeing with the boy.
"What a wondrous night this is!"
the lad sang out with joy.

They made their way to Bethlehem
and found the manger stall.
A few had gathered quietly to
see the baby small.

The brothers walked on velvet feet
and gazed upon the one
Whom God had sent to bless the
earth, His precious Holy Son.

Jesus—oh, how wonderful to
see him sleeping there;
In all the world the brothers
three had seen no face so fair.

"Is he very beautiful?"
asked Josh so quietly.
In a moment Mary realized
he could not see.

She looked at Joseph and he smiled,
and in this holy place
She said, "Josh, come nearer, lad,
and touch the baby's face."

Josh was led unto the
crib in which the baby lay.
His hand reached out and
trembled just a bit above
the hay.

He touched the tiny face, and
happy tears sprang to his eyes.
He raised his head and suddenly
he saw the starlit skies!

He saw his brothers at the door,
the ones he loved so much.
He saw the Mother and the Holy
Child she let him touch.

He sobbed aloud with joy and
ran unto the brothers three.
He threw his arms around them
and shouted, "I can see!"

When the brothers realized the
boy had gained his sight,
They danced for joy and sang
aloud, "This is a glorious night!"

The little shepherd spoke once
more unto the Mother mild,
"Oh, thank you! What a gift it
was to touch the
Holy Child."

"Come," said Reuben, "it is to our
mother we must go.
Not a moment longer must she wait
the news to know!"

Mira was not sleeping when she heard
the happy song
Of her four sons on their way home;
for her the night was long.

She could not sleep but waited for the
morning sun to rise.
Now her sons were home again, but
with a great surprise.

"Mother, Mother!" came the happy
shout from down the street.
The neighbors' doors were opening,
this happy voice to greet.

Mira's son was in her arms
and shouting merrily,
"Mother, oh dear Mother, do
you know that I can see?"

Mira was astonished as she
took in every word.
Could her prayers be answered?
Had a miracle occurred?

She held her breath and looked
with hope into his shining eyes,
And then she saw reflected there
a glimpse of Paradise.

"It's true!" said Reuben joyfully.
"God's Son was born this night,
And in God's mercy, He has
given Josh the gift of sight."

The village folk had
gathered 'round, the
wondrous news to hear.
The brothers told the
story as their mother
held Josh near.

"Jesus Christ, the
Son of God, has come
to men on earth.
Let us praise our
God on high,
for this our
Savior's birth!"

As we lift our vision clear
to see this starlit night,
Imagining so long ago the
one that shone so bright,

The song this tiny shepherd
knew can still be heard today,
That led him without seeing
eyes to where the baby lay.

God, the Mighty Shepherd,
longs to share His grand design,
And dreams for every soul that
breathes to find a faith that's blind;

That He may send His healing
touch to fill each heart with joy,
Just as He did in Bethlehem for
this small shepherd boy.

Author **Kay Hall** is an actress and an award-winning composer. She was awarded first place in the National Music Composition Award for The American Way. An accomplished pianist, she graduated Summa Cum Laude with a Master of Music Degree from Georgia State University. Kay is a member of the Atlanta Writers Club. *The Little Blind Shepherd* is one of her many accomplishments in the children's book genre.